What Is Providence?

Basics of the Reformed Faith

How Do We Glorify God?
How Our Children Come to Faith
What Are Election and Predestination?
What Is a Reformed Church?
What Is a True Calvinist?
What Is Biblical Preaching?
What Is Justification by Faith Alone?
What Is Perseverance of the Saints?
What Is Providence?
What Is the Christian Worldview?
What Is the Lord's Supper?
What Is Spiritual Warfare?
What Is True Conversion?
Why Do We Baptize Infants?

What Is Providence?

DEREK W. H. THOMAS

P&R PUBLISHING
P.O. BOX 817 • PHILLIPSBURG • NEW JERSEY 08865-0817

Page design by Tobias Design

Printed in the United States of America

Library of Congress Cataloging-in-Publication Data

Thomas, Derek, 1953–
What is providence? / Derek W.H. Thomas.
    p. cm. — (Basics of the reformed faith)
Includes bibliographical references.
ISBN 978-1-59638-092-9
1. Providence and government of God—Christianity. I. Title.
BT135.T46 2008
231'.5—dc22
                                      2008022061

■Few things distinguish Christian and secular worldviews with greater clarity than the doctrine of providence. This doctrine insists that everything (yes, *everything*) that happens does so because God wills it to happen, wills it to happen *before* it happens, wills it to happen *in the way* that it happens.[1] Such a view signals immediately that history is not arbitrary or fortuitous; neither is it "simple determinism," "*Que Sera, Sera*" or, "whatever will be, will be," as though our own choices and involvement have no relevance whatsoever, a fatalistic view more reflective of Islam than biblical Christianity.

So central is the doctrine of providence that summary accounts of Christian doctrine, such as the Westminster Shorter Catechism, raise the issue at the very beginning. Thus, question 11 of the Shorter Catechism asks: "What are God's works of providence?" To which the answer is given: "God's works of providence are, his most holy, wise, and powerful preserving and governing all his creatures, and all their actions."

The key word is "all," signaling the totality of God's control over the world in which we live. Our Father in heaven takes care of his own children, ensuring that his purposes for them will be accomplished despite the forces of sin and evil designed to oppose and frustrate his intentions. In the end, everything occurs according to the will of God.

All this can sound either scary or reassuring depending on our frame of reference. For Christians, at least those who are not preoccupied with philosophical questions, this is a most glorious truth because it is the basis upon which we can be certain that heaven will be ours! It only requires one errant molecule in the universe to question the certainty of the future and unless we can be assured that *everything* is submissive to God's sovereign rule, there is always the possibility that the future may not be as we have believed it to be. Of course, Christians don't always think like this. The idea of God's sovereignty seems to threaten human freedom and contingency. "What about free will?" is a question that frequently lies near the surface, erupting with volcanic force and, if the logic is followed, threatening all possibility of certainty about anything and everything!

The word *providence* consists of a prefix, *pro*, meaning "in front of" or "before," and the Latin root *videre*, "to see." Words, of course, do not always mean what their etymology suggests, and in this case, "to see beforehand," suggesting foreknowledge, is not what is intended by the word *providence*. Providence suggests God's care of the world, both his supervision of all events and circumstances *and* his provision for all of our needs. It is more than God's ability to "see" into the future; it is his *active* and *determined* care to ensure that what he has promised for us actually does come to pass.

The alternatives to this robust notion of providence are: God can see the future he desires but is powerless to bring it about (no control), or that he can see all "possible" futures based on the free choices of individuals without determining one solely based on his own volition (another form of no control), or that his control is a general one only and not one where the individual details are determined in any way (limited control). Some will recognize various strands of theological and philosophical ideology in these alternatives, both ancient and modern, but before we examine these it will prove helpful to examine the issue biblically and theologically.

PROVIDENCE AND THE BIBLE

The Bible gives us many examples of God's providential ordering of the details and circumstances of the lives of individuals. These tangible, visible demonstrations of his providence encourage us that just as he worked in the lives of certain people in the past, so he is able to work in the present. We must draw conclusions from these accounts with considerable care, lest we misconstrue those things which are unique to these individuals and their precise location within the history of redemption. Such accounts are not necessarily meant to imply that we can expect God to work in our lives *in exactly the same way*.[2] However, seeing the way God worked in the lives of others, sensitive as we must be to what may be unique and what may be considered more general and timeless in their significance, should prompt us to recall Paul's words regarding Israel in the time of the wilderness wanderings: "these things took place as examples for us" (1 Cor. 10:6). We will, therefore, examine three examples from the Bible to help us understand the meaning of God's providence: the stories of Ruth and her mother-in-law, Naomi, Joseph, and Job.

Naomi and Ruth

The book of Ruth is that tiny jewel that sparkles after the darkness of the book of Judges, a book which ends with the somber words, "everyone did what was right in his own eyes" (Judg. 21:25). It is a refrain picked up from an earlier statement in the book: "In those days there was no king in Israel. Everyone did what was right in his own eyes" (Judg. 17:6). From such dark surroundings emerges something that, in one sense at least, is wholly unexpected; but only to those unfamiliar with the ways of God!

The book of Ruth is illustrative of the doctrine of providence from two distinct points of view: a macrocosmic level in which we begin to see how the purposes of God announced in the Garden of Eden are fulfilled—that the woman's "offspring" is set at enmity with the serpent's "offspring"—the so-called *proto-evangelium* (Gen. 3:15). This is the story of the Old Testament, from Genesis to Malachi. It tells us how the flow of redemptive history from the patriarchs to the prophets is one in which the line of the Messiah is told. This is what enabled Jesus to lead the two disciples on the Emmaus road on a Bible study from "Moses and all the Prophets," pointing out to them "the things concerning himself" (Luke 24:27). Had the story line of the Old Testament not displayed a unifying theme established by divine providence, this would not have been possible. God has ensured that his promise of salvation to sinners through the atoning work of his own Son be realized, not through haphazard events contingent upon the choices of men and women and the forces of evil over which God has no ultimate control, but by events that are planned and certain. There is a master-plan! God reigns through the stumbling, hobbling service of his people and the rage and malice of his foes to establish his eternal purpose for this world. The story of a small, insignificant family from Bethlehem is one of the building blocks in the coming of Jesus Christ into the world. A son born to Ruth and her husband, Boaz, becomes King David's grandfather![3]

The story of Ruth is also illustrative of the doctrine of providence at a microcosmic level. It shows us God's wise provision of a husband for a Moabite widow—which, in Bethlehem in those times was a necessary provision to ensure her release from a life of penury! When, by God's astonishing grace, Ruth professed her faith in her mother-in-law's God, thereby evidencing a work of conversion in her heart, she also vowed to go with Naomi to Bethlehem. There were no guarantees for her there as a Moabite widow, which is partly why Naomi had urged her to return to her own people (Ruth 1:8-9). She did not know that God would provide for her in a way that would be a source of wonderment forever afterwards. In the words of the English poet William Cowper:

> God moves in a mysterious way
> His wonders to perform;
> He plants his footsteps in the sea
> And rides upon the storm.[4]

The problem, of course, with planting footsteps in the sea is that liquids do not retain their shape once the foot is withdrawn! In other words, the ways of God cannot always be discerned by us in any visible, transparent way. It requires from us a degree of trust and faith in the providence of God. In ways that only *afterwards* became clearer, Ruth's gleaning in the barley fields of Bethlehem was part of God's plan all along whereby she and Boaz would meet and eventually marry and have a child called Obed, "the father of Jesse, the father of David" (Ruth 4:17). On a microcosmic scale, Ruth could express wonder in the providence (provision!) of God in her time of need. As the Puritan John Flavel put it: "Sometimes providences, like Hebrew letters, must be read backward."5

On a macrocosmic scale, she knew next to nothing of her role in the fulfillment of God's promise in the Garden of Eden. On this level, there were aspects of what God did in her life that only future generations would understand. And give glory to God!

Joseph

The entire life of Joseph is summarized in Genesis 50:20: "As for you, you meant evil against me, but God meant it for good." The teenager we met at the beginning of the story is now over a hundred years old. His life has come full circle and he is addressing his duplicitous brothers. Their action, in selling him into slavery, had nothing but evil intent written all over it. Their malevolence can in no way be lessened by the knowledge that things did not turn out as they might have done. Truth is, God overruled their evil actions to accomplish a purpose that neither they nor Joseph could have fathomed. God brought *good* out of evil. In the words of the Westminster Confession, God in providence "doth uphold, direct, dispose and govern all creatures, actions and things" to bring about a sovereignly predetermined plan.[6]

This predetermined plan God accomplished through a complicated strategy which initially did not yield confidence of a good outcome. Joseph's descent into slavery followed by a false accusation of rape resulting in a lengthy imprisonment, spelled his downward spiral to the bottom. His life could hardly have been much worse. Only later, from the vantage point of what God had, in fact, accomplished—ensuring that an heir of the covenant promises was in the most powerful position in Egypt at a time when famine engulfed Canaan thereby ensuring the survival of the covenant family—could Joseph look back and see the hand of God. It took faith on Joseph's part to learn this lesson, and—in Shakespeare's words—to discover:

> There's a divinity that shapes our ends,
> Rough-hew them how we will.[7]

The metaphor Shakespeare employs is taken from the ancient practice of cutting hedgerows. The practice involved two people, one cutting roughly and quickly and another following along afterwards doing detailed trimming and shaping. Joseph, to say the very least, has been rough-hewing, but God has shaped his own design. Looking at things from God's perspective, we see a wisdom that is incomparable and majestic. No matter how dark things get, his hand is always in control. Or, as the poet William Cowper wrote in the hymn cited earlier:

Judge not the Lord by feeble sense
But trust him for his grace;
Behind a frowning providence
He hides a smiling face.

His purposes will ripen fast;
Unfolding every hour.
The bud may have a bitter taste,
But sweet will be the flower.

Providence has wider issues in mind than merely our personal comfort or gain. In response to the oft-cited question in times of difficulty, "Why *me*?" the answer that the narrative gives is, "*Them!*" He allows us to suffer so that *others* may be blessed. Joseph suffered in order that his undeserving brothers might receive blessing. In their case, they would be kept alive during a time of famine and have the covenant promises of their father, grandfather, and great-grandfather reaffirmed before their eyes.

What do you think went through the minds of those disciples who carried the blood-soaked body of Stephen to his burial? Were they perhaps tempted to say, "What a waste! Couldn't God have spared this godly man so that he might be of use to the church in her time of need? Does God care about us at all?" In all these questions, they would have been showing the short-sightedness that is so much a part of unbelief. They would not have been reckoning on the purposes of God. For there, at the feet of Stephen's corpse, stood a man upon whom Stephen's death had the most profound impact. In hearing the voice of Jesus speak to him and accuse him of persecuting *him* (i.e., Jesus), Paul learned what is arguably the most characteristic feature of his later writings: to persecute one of Jesus' little ones is to persecute Jesus himself, because every Christian is united to Jesus Christ in an indissoluble union!

And what were the purposes behind Joseph's suffering? As with the story of Ruth, at least two are forthcoming. First, Joseph learned that whatever happened to him personally, he was part of a larger purpose in which God's plan was being revealed. In that case, he could not hold grudges against his brothers, no matter how badly they had behaved. True, they must learn their sin and confess it; this explains the lengthy way in which Joseph finally reveals himself to them as his brother after first making them think that they had stolen from the prince of Egypt. God used him as an instrument in the spiritual growth of his brothers, and Joseph shows his sense of this by his unwillingness to hold a grudge against them. No matter what personal hurt he had experienced, God was working in the lives of his brothers, for which he could only be thankful.

But secondly, and on a much larger scale, Joseph begins to learn the answer to the question, How will the promises made to Abraham be fulfilled? At one level, the final scene of Jacob's burial in Canaan attended by a huge entourage of Egyptians seems a curious way to end the story of Joseph.

And Pharaoh answered, "Go up, and bury your father, as he made you swear." So Joseph went up to bury his father. With him went up all the servants of Pharaoh, the elders of his household, and all the elders of the land of Egypt, as well as all the household of Joseph, his brothers, and his father's household. Only their children, their flocks, and their herds were left in the land of Goshen. And there went up with him both chariots and horsemen. It was a very great company. (Gen. 50:6-9)

Why is Moses telling us that the Egyptians went with Joseph and his family to bury his father, Jacob? He wants us to understand that in the end, the Egyptians are paying homage to Joseph's family! When Jacob makes his son pledge to bury him in the land of promise (see Gen. 50:5), he is remembering the promise that God had given to Abraham of a land—a land that at this time they did not possess apart from this burial plot! At the end of Genesis the people of God are nowhere near possessing Canaan. They are going to spend four hundred years in captivity in Egypt. But in Jacob's burial there is a glimpse of things to come. God has not forgotten his promise. *He never does!*

Job

There is no book in the Bible quite like the book of Job. It is a tale of a man who loses everything: his ten children, his entire fortune and eventually his health. It is not a tale of a *wicked* man who suffers incalculable loss, in which case we might be able to justify it as a tale of someone receiving his just deserts. No! Three times we are informed at the very outset that Job was "blameless and upright, one who feared God and turned away from evil"

(Job 1:1, 8; 2:3). This is not a case of "Why do bad things happen to *bad* people?" Such circumstances are in part explained by recourse to God's justice. The question that looms large in the opening chapter of the book of Job is of another kind altogether: Why do bad things happen to *godly* people? The sheer extent of Job's suffering seems to call into question something at the very heart of God himself.

It is not possible to resort to a solution that identifies Satan as the cause of all evil in the universe, thereby removing God from any involvement and culpability, because in the story of Job, it is God who seems firmly in charge of the ensuing events. It is God who summons Satan into his presence to give an account of his doings (Job 1:6). Additionally, it is at the Lord's suggestion that Job is made a target for Satan's attention: "Have you considered my servant Job?" (Job 1:8; 2:3). It is the dilemma that the prophet Amos poses: "Does disaster come to a city, unless the LORD has done it?" (Amos 3:6). It clearly was the way Job viewed it: "Have mercy on me, have mercy on me, O you my friends, for the hand of God has touched me!" (Job 19:21).

The "solution" that God is good but not sovereign, though resorted to frequently, was not one that sounded plausible to Job. This, according to Rabbi Harold Kushner, was Job's problem. In his famous book written in 1981, *When Bad Things Happen to Good People*, he wrote: "God wants the righteous to live peaceful, happy lives, but sometimes even He can't bring that about. It is too difficult even for God to keep cruelty and chaos from claiming their innocent victims."[8] More recently, in an increasingly popular view known as Open Theism, similar views have been expressed limiting God's power in an attempt to maintain human freedom. Gregory Boyd, for example, has written, "God must work with, and battle against, other created beings. While none of these beings can ever match God's own power, each has some degree of genuine influence within the cosmos."9

According to these views, when Job concluded, "Naked I came from my mother's womb, and naked shall I return. The LORD gave, and the LORD has taken away; blessed be the name of the LORD" (Job 1:21), and, "Shall we receive good from God, and shall we not receive evil?" (Job 2:10), he was wrong to attribute his suffering to the sovereignty of God! But to be more consistent with the data of Scripture we must conclude that in the traumatic war between God and "cosmic powers" (Eph. 6:12) in which Christians are often the battleground, Satan must get permission to touch one of God's own children (Job 1:12; 2:6; Luke 22:31-32). Whatever problems arise (and genuine problems do arise), a "solution" posed at the expense of God's sovereignty is one that fails to do justice to the data of Scripture. Affliction, to be sure, is God's "strange" work: "he does not willingly afflict or grieve the children of men" (Lam. 3:33). But affliction *is* something that God afflicts upon his people.

In the end, Job is never given an explanation for his suffering other than that it is beyond him to comprehend. He is reduced to laying his hand over his mouth as a sign of his submission to a higher will that he must trust even when he does not understand (Job 40:4). Nowhere does God say to him that the desperate circumstances in which he found himself were outside of God's control to change, that he must consider the complexity of the supernatural world in which powerful forces of darkness are at work and to which even the sovereign God must yield. At no point does God abdicate his rule. He never takes his hand away from the tiller. He remains in control even in the darkest of circumstances.

TAKING THE HIGH ROAD

There are, considered simply, three views of divine providence that seek to maintain a high view of God's sovereignty in providence: the classical or Augustinian-Calvinistic view, the "Arminian" or *simple divine foreknowledge* view, and the view known as Molinism.

The classical view, held by theologians of the caliber of Augustine, Anselm, Aquinas, Luther, Calvin, and Edwards, maintains that everything that occurs, both good and evil, falls out according to a predetermined plan of almighty God. God knows what will occur in the future because he has predetermined it. Such a view not only affirms an exhaustive divine foreknowledge on God's part, including the voluntary actions of human beings; it also insists that such foreknowledge is impossible unless God has also predetermined the future. In the words of Jonathan Edwards, if God knows something *before* it occurs, "then it is impossible it should ever be otherwise," adding, "this is the same thing as to say, it is impossible but that the event should come to pass: and this is the same as to say that its coming to pass is *necessary*."[10]

This view is the *classical* view of providence. It assumes God's exhaustive foreknowledge and infinite power to accomplish his immutable purpose. Put summarily, this view of providence asserts, "there is no erratic power, or action, or motion in creatures, but that they are governed by God's secret plan in such a way that nothing happens except what is knowingly and willingly decreed by him."[11]

Alternatively, there are two views which seek to uphold aspects of God's sovereignty (either his power or his foresight, or both) while maintaining a "genuine" view of human freedom and power to choose in any possible context. Both of these views seek to retain *some form of theistic control and foreknowledge*, but at the expense of an element of "risk" on God's part. The outcome in both cases is not *altogether* certain from God's point of view. In varying degrees, both of these views share in common the prioritizing of human freedom in such a way that "free acts" are solely determined by the person's will. Human freedom involves, according to this view, the *power of contrary choice* such that, in precisely the same circumstances an alternative outcome *could have been chosen* thereby altering the course of events.

Whereas in the classical view, God foreknows because he foreordains, in the second view (sometimes known as *simple divine foreknowledge*), God foreordains *because* he foreknows. The relationship between God's will in determining the future and man's response is entirely reversed. God chooses on the basis of a certain choice made by man. At a stroke, this (it is claimed) preserves genuine human choice (freedom), and provides a better solution to the problem of evil (locating it in genuine human freedom rather than the will of God). This view (associated with Jacob Arminius) is most clearly expressed by William Hasker: "It is clear that God's foreknowledge cannot be used either to *bring about* the occurrence of a foreknown event or to *prevent* such an event from occurring. . . . In the logical order of dependence of events, one might say, by the 'time' God knows something will happen, it is 'too late' either to *bring about* its happening or to *prevent* it from happening."[12] It should be immediately obvious that this view *limits* God's freedom and power.

Enter "Middle Knowledge"

We have presented two views of providence: the *classical* view involving a "no risk" strategy on God's part in which every event that occurs does so because God has willed it to occur, and the *simple divine foreknowledge* view which subsumes God's sovereignty beneath human freedom, preserving divine foreknowledge at the expense of limiting divine sovereignty. Seeing the implications for divine sovereignty, and the need to preserve human freedom, the sixteenth-century Jesuit theologian, Luis de Molina (1535-1600), proposed an alternative model involving the concept of "middle knowledge," eponymously known as Molinism.[13]

Put simply, middle knowledge affirms that in addition to *necessary truths* (truths like arithmetic or logic) and *free knowledge* (things that are true because God wills them—that in 2007, Jackson is the capital of Mississippi and the Boston Red Sox are the World Series champions in baseball), there are things which are *possibly* true—and *would be true* under certain circumstances. Had I not procrastinated in writing this booklet which you are now reading, it would have been in the editor's hands several months ago. Had I remained in Belfast in 1996 instead of accepting a call to teach at a seminary in the United States, my son would not now be living in the United States.

Such *possible* outcomes are anticipated in the Bible itself: one passage made use of by both Molina and current advocates of Open Theism is Matthew 11:20-24. Jesus told the citizens of Bethsaida and Chorazin, towns in which mighty works had been performed but with no resulting faith, that *if* these same works had been done in Tyre and Sidon, they *would have* repented. This is not a statement of what actually happened but of what *would have happened under certain circumstances*. It is an example of middle knowledge. Thus Molinism suggests that God knows *all* such possible outcomes or worlds. From this infinite array of possibilities, God wills the actual world that you and I know.

Defenders of the classical view of providence do not dispute that God knows all possible outcomes. It is a corollary of his omniscience. What Molinism asserts, however, is that God "chooses" (actualizes) the world (out of an infinite set of possibilities) in which men and women make the *free* choices they make. Of these possible worlds, he chooses the one we now know and experience. As William Lane Craig, a defender of middle knowledge, puts it:

> Since God knows what any free creature would do in any situation, he can by creating the appropriate situations, bring it about that creatures will achieve ends and purposes, and that they will do so *freely*.[14]

The problem with this view is that if in any given set of circumstances there exists an actual possibility that one may choose *differently*—something which is necessary if human freedom is to be maintained—it is not possible to predict what one may choose, and therefore it is not possible for God to actualize the total outcome without infringing upon the freedom of the individual to choose.[15]

So far, even though we have maintained that Arminians and Molinists are in error as regards a biblical view of providence, they do have a high view of providence and share many of the beliefs of those who maintain a classical view of providence. More recently, however, another view of providence has emerged, one which abandons the traditional understanding of God's foreknowledge. It is known as Open Theism (or Openness Theology). This view maintains that God is not omniscient. Given that Molinism fails to maintain human indeterminism (at some level, God still makes a "choice" of which set of possible truths to actuate), Open Theists have abandoned the claim that God knows the future in its entirety. Instead, they affirm that "God knows everything about the future which it is logically possible for him to know."[16] Instead of adopting the view that God knows all possible futures, Open Theists claim (rightly) that if absolute human freedom is maintained, the future cannot be known with absolute certainty. God knows the past and present perfectly and exhaustively. But he *cannot* on this basis know the future *in the same way*.

Not only does Open Theism deny the traditional understanding of God's exhaustive knowledge; it also denies the traditional understanding of God's power. As one of the best-known advocates of Open Theism puts it: "God must work with, and battle against, other created beings. While none of these beings can ever match God's own power, each has some degree of genuine influence within the cosmos."[17] To see where this view takes us, we should note the same author's interpretation of the sufferings of Job: "it was the *satan*, not God who afflicted Job. True God entered into the wager with the *satan* and allowed him to afflict Job in order to answer the *satan's* assault on his integrity. In this sense he brought Job's troubles upon him. But he did not himself plan or cause these afflictions, as Job later alleges. . . . What happens to Job certainly is not part of God's perfect plan for his life."[18] God is at the mercy of the evil forces within the cosmos (and even the cosmos itself), and the only reassurance we have is that his power is greater than theirs. There can be, however, no guarantee that a final victory will be forthcoming, only optimism based on past experience of God's victories.[19] Such a view may uphold genuine human freedom, but at the expense of a radical alteration in our traditional understanding of God.

THE BIBLICAL EVIDENCE

What is the biblical evidence for the classical view of providence that God is in absolute control of the past, present, *and future*? The evidence is substantial:

1) *The sovereignty of God over the entire creation.* Having created the universe, he continues to uphold it: "For by him all things were created. . . . And in him all things hold together" (Col. 1:16-17).

2) *God exercises a divine plan in creation.* "Whatever the LORD pleases, he does, in heaven and on earth, in the seas and all deeps" (Ps. 135:6).

3) *God's sovereignty extends over individuals—even wicked ones.* Speaking of the Pharaoh of Egypt, God says through Moses, "But for this purpose I have raised you up, to show you my power, so that my name may be proclaimed in all the earth" (Ex. 9:16). Even in the matter of the hardening of Pharaoh's heart, the Bible insists that this, too, was God's doing (Ex. 9:12; cf. 4:21; 10:20; 11:10).

4) *God's sovereignty extends to "chance" events.* "The lot is cast into the lap, but its every decision is from the LORD" (Prov. 16:33).

5) *God is sovereign over the most wicked events.* In the crucifixion of Jesus, Peter pronounced on the day of Pentecost that at one level it had been because of the wickedness of the unbelieving Jews in Jerusalem; at the same time, it was "according to the definite plan and foreknowledge of God" (Acts 2:23). And the prophet Isaiah declared: "I am the LORD, and there is no other. I form light and create darkness, I make well-being and create calamity, I am the LORD, who does all these things" (Isa. 45:6-7).

6) *God is sovereign in the lives of his people before they are brought into existence.* The psalmist declares that "Your eyes saw my unformed substance; in your book were written,

every one of them, the days that were formed for me, when as yet there were none of them" (Ps. 139:16).

7) *God's sovereignty ensures that predictive prophecy in the Bible can be trusted.* Open Theists especially are vulnerable at this point. If God cannot know the future exhaustively (at best, all that can be known by us and God is a trajectory of expectation based on statistical data from past and present examples), then our traditional understanding of prophecy—a guarantee that a certain outcome will eventuate based on God's immutable covenant and exhaustive power to ensure its fulfillment—is suspect. When God makes a promise to Abraham and repeats it to his progeny—for example, "all this land that I have promised" (Ex. 32:13; cf. Gen. 15:13, 18; 28:15)—the certainty of its fulfillment cannot be guaranteed apart from a traditional view of prophecy. This includes such prophecies as the incarnation of the Savior to his Second Coming, for neither are *guarantees* apart from a consideration of the total sovereignty of God to bring them about.

8) *God's sovereignty as traditionally understood is a necessary corollary of the gospel.* For the gospel to be "good news" there must be some certainty that there is victory— over sin, over death, over Satan. In the case of Open Theism, there can be no certainty that some malevolent spirit will not rise up and seriously undermine the victory achieved at the cross. And in the case of Arminianism, too much credit is given to the autonomy of human decision to ensure that any gospel offered will be chosen. For the Bible also asserts with equal conviction that the "natural

man"—the unconverted individual in union with Adam—is so wrought upon by the effects of sin in his mind, affections *and will*, that he not only *will not* but *cannot* choose the good that is offered to him. "For the mind that is set on the flesh is hostile to God, for it does not submit to God's law; indeed, it cannot. Those who are in the flesh cannot please God" (Rom. 8:7-8). As Jesus put it, "No one can come to me unless the Father who sent me draws him" (John 6:44).

The evidence is impressively expansive and touches on some of the most difficult issues, including the area of suffering and the wider issue of evil itself.

PROVIDENCE AND SUFFERING

In all three cases cited above—the circumstances of Joseph in Egypt, Naomi and Ruth in Moab and Bethlehem, and Job in the land of Uz—the distribution of calamity appears to be somewhat haphazard, perhaps, we might even say, capricious. *That* is the problem that we face in relation to the doctrine of providence. How do we maintain the goodness of God when it appears as though evil things happen not simply "under his watch," but according to *his* plan!

The problem arises in relation to creation itself. The world is out of joint; it has been "subjected to futility" (Rom. 8:20) and consequently is "groaning . . . in the pains of childbirth" (Rom. 8:22). It "suffers" though it has not sinned. It was Adam who sinned in the Garden of Eden, and the ground is cursed because of his failure:

25

"cursed is the ground because of you" (Gen. 3:17). It suffers because of its identification with Adam just as it will experience an emancipation from its present "bondage" (Rom. 8:21) in the creation of the new heavens and new earth by the Second Adam (Isa. 65:17; 66:22; 2 Peter 3:13).

The problem also arises with respect to what is sometimes called "innocent suffering." We may insist, in the case of human beings, that it is *never* the case that the innocent suffer for in reality it is always sinners who suffer and that the claim to innocence can only be made with any integrity in the case of Jesus. He *never* sinned and yet was subject to the hostility not only of Satan and the world of sinners, but also to the unmitigated fury of God's retributive righteousness on the cross. This has in recent days given rise to some serious misgivings about such an interpretation of the cross—that the suffering of one who is innocent is inherently unfair and calls into question the integrity of God's providence with respect to his Son.[20] But this is to misunderstand the nature and purpose of substitution. At the moment of judgment, when God's righteous indignation falls upon his Son on the cross and Jesus is heard to repeat the God-forsakenness of the psalmist, "My God, my God, why have you forsaken me?" (Ps. 22:1; cf. Matt. 27:46; Mark 15:34), Jesus is *not* innocent; he has assumed the place of the wicked. As the substitute he dies *for* the righteous, and what he receives is justice—perfect and appropriate justice.

But *innocent* suffering cannot be dismissed simply by a consideration of the fact that the world in which we live is under the curse (Gen. 3:17). Job's suffering is a dilemma precisely because he is introduced to us—*by God himself*—as a *godly* man (Job 1:8; 2:3). Similarly, the blind man healed by Jesus in John 9 had been blind from birth. His condition prompted the question from Jesus' disciples, "Rabbi, who sinned, this man or his parents, that he was born blind?" (John 9:2). True, even at birth, this man had inherited the guilt of Adam's transgression: "sin came into the world through one man, and death through sin, and so death spread to all men because all sinned" (Rom. 5:12).[21]

This, however, is not the line Jesus takes in his response. Rather, he tells the disciples that this man's suffering was for an instructional purpose: "It was not that this man sinned, or his parents, but that the works of God might be displayed in him" (John 9:3). This reply does not deny the man's sinfulness or that of his parents; the point at issue is that neither contributed to the fact of his blindness. The reason for his condition lies outside of these considerations, fulfilling the Bible's "law of harvest": suffering comes upon one in order that blessing might come upon another, according to the principle, "unless a grain of wheat falls into the earth and dies, it remains alone; but if it dies, it bears much fruit" (John 12:24). There is no doubt that this man's suffering and consequent healing, not to mention the story of Job's recovery, proves of enormous encouragement to us. We read these stories and we see the hand of God at work in their lives. True enough, they do not necessarily experience what we might have expected, but in each case there is the reassurance that what happens to them is not merely the product of chance or good fortune, or the ingenuity of the individual in making good choices.

PROVIDENCE AND SIN

To the questions "How did sin originate?" and "Why has God permitted it?" there can be no final answer that will satisfy every possible nuance. To the latter question, the most promising avenue is the answer that suggests that God had a good reason for doing so. God created Adam and Eve in such a way that they sinned. What possible reason did God have for doing so? The answer must lie along the lines that *some greater good would be forthcoming, a good that would not be forthcoming had there been no sin in the world*. It is a view classically stated by Augustine:

> For the Almighty God, who, as even the heathen acknowledge, has supreme power over all things, being Himself supremely good, would never permit the existence of anything evil among His works if He were not so omnipotent and good that He can bring good even out of evil.[22]

Whatever the merits of this argument, the fact is that God does coordinate all events and circumstances to bring about good. It is the testimony of the well-known passage in Romans 8: "for those who love God all things work together for good" (Rom. 8:28). As C. H. Spurgeon has written on this verse:

> Upon some points a believer is absolutely sure. He knows, for instance, that God sits in the stern-sheets of the vessel when it rocks most. He believes that an invisible hand is always on the world's tiller, and that wherever providence may drift, Jehovah steers it.

That re-assuring knowledge prepares him for everything. He looks over the raging waters and sees the spirit of Jesus treading the billows, and he hears a voice saying, "It is I, be not afraid." He knows too that God is always wise, and, knowing this, he is confident that there can be no accidents, no mistakes; that nothing can occur which ought not to arise. He can say, "If I should lose all I have, it is better that I should lose than have, if God so wills: the worst calamity is the wisest and the kindest thing that could befall to me if God ordains it." "We know that all things work together for good to them that love God." The Christian does not merely hold this as a theory, but he knows it as a matter of fact. Everything has worked for good as yet; the poisonous drugs mixed in fit proportions have worked the cure; the sharp cuts of the lancet have cleansed out the proud flesh and facilitated the healing. Every event as yet has worked out the most divinely blessed results; and so, believing that God rules all, that he governs wisely, that he brings good out of evil, the believer's heart is assured, and he is enabled calmly to meet each trial as it comes. The believer can in the spirit of true resignation pray, "Send me what thou wilt, my God, so long as it comes from thee; never came there an ill portion from thy table to any of thy children."[23]

PROVIDENCE AND HUMAN RESPONSIBILITY

Given the high view of divine sovereignty in the classical formulation of providence, it is easy for us to slip into a kind of determinism or fatalism with regard to human responsibility. *"Que sera, sera"* ("whatever will be, will be") sang Doris Day in Alfred Hitchcock's 1956 film *The Man Who Knew Too Much*, and like the song, Christians can "know too much"—or think they know too much—about God's sovereignty that they justify all kinds of neglect (failing to study for an exam, leaving late for a meeting) by advocating that this is the will of God. The response of Scripture to this kind of thinking is swift and decisive: "Through sloth the roof sinks in, and through indolence the house leaks" (Eccl. 10:18). "The sluggard does not plow in the autumn; he will seek at harvest and have nothing" (Prov. 20:4). These passages urge upon us the most ardent effort to ensure that we do not neglect our responsibility.

In the fourth chapter of Acts, Peter and John are being threatened by the Jewish Sanhedrin not to preach or teach in the name of Jesus Christ. When the two reported the matter to the other disciples, they collectively raised the issue before God in prayer:

> "Sovereign Lord," they said, "who made the heaven and the earth and the sea and everything in them. . . . both Herod and Pontius Pilate, along with the Gentiles and the peoples of Israel, [did] whatever your hand and your plan had predestined to take place." (Acts 4:24-28)

They certainly believed in a high view of God's sovereignty and predetermination in what was an evil circumstance. But what are they doing with this information? Resigning themselves to a form of fatalistic paralysis? No! They are urgently beseeching the God of heaven to hear them and grant them boldness in their decision of non-compliance: "look upon their threats and grant to your servants to continue to speak your word with all boldness" (Acts 4:29). Their belief in God's sovereignty (why else would we pray?) made them all the more bold to act. There is no hint in the New Testament that belief in divine sovereignty led to inertia and indecision. As Jerry Bridges puts it:

> Prayer assumes the sovereignty of God. If God is not sovereign, we have no assurance that He is able to answer our prayers. Our prayers would become nothing more than wishes. But while God's sovereignty, along with His wisdom and love, is the foundation of our trust in Him, prayer is the expression of trust.[24]

Theologians and philosophers have coined the word "compatibilism" to describe this relationship between divine sovereignty and human responsibility. Both are true and both need equal stress. C. S. Lewis explained it this way:

> In the play Hamlet, Ophelia climbs out on a branch overhanging a river: the branch breaks, she falls and drowns. What would you reply if someone asked, "Did Ophelia die because Shakespeare, for poetic reasons, wanted her to die at that moment—or because the branch broke?" I think that one would have to say, "For both reasons." Every event in the play happens as a result of other events in the play, but also every event happens because the poet wants it to happen. All the events in the play are Shakespearean events; similarly, all events in the

real world are providential events. . . . "Providence" and Natural causation are not alternatives; both determine every event because both are one.[25]

TRUSTING GOD

In the end, the doctrine of God's providence is a call for us to trust in God. Take, for example, the case of Jacob.

There are few more poignant words in the Bible than the despair-laden response of Jacob to his sons' news that their half-brother, Simeon, had been taken captive in Egypt. "All this has come against me," he cried (Gen. 42:36). Poor Jacob!

He thought his favorite son, Joseph, was dead. *He wasn't!*

He thought his next favorite son, Simeon, was as good as dead. *He wasn't!*

He thought that any hope of famine-relief from the Egyptians (given that incriminating evidence pointed to the fact that Jacob's sons had dealt treacherously with the Egyptians) was doomed to failure. *It wasn't!*

Based on the solid empirical evidence at his disposal, thinking rationally and *without reference to the power of God*, Jacob came to the conclusion, echoed by Dante's *Inferno*, as Virgil leads Dante through the gates of Hell, marked by the haunting inscription, "ABANDON ALL HOPE, YOU WHO ENTER HERE."[26] It was all perfectly reasonable. And it was all perfectly wrong!

Jacob's despair is one we identify with—all too read-ily: that which we *see*, or *hear*, or *touch*, or can *reason about* says one thing to us. But such analysis fails to take into consideration the perspective identified by the Puritans as *sub specie aeternitatis*—a resolve to look *upwards*, to view things in the light of the heavenly realm, of *eternity*! To put the matter simply, Jacob reasoned from a perspective of practical atheism! He failed to take God into account. The truth was that Joseph was not only alive; he was the Prime Minister of Egypt! His sons, though guilty of many things and capable of blatant hypocrisy, were not guilty of treachery in their dealings with the Egyptians. And Simeon was in good hands, under the careful supervision of his brother Joseph (even though he didn't know it).

God was at work in the details of Jacob's life—yes, *in the details*, even though we foolishly repeat the axiom that the 'devil is in the details.' God loves details! It is in the details that we discern his hand of providence—ruling, di-recting, providing, sustaining, preventing, surprising. What may look catastrophic from one point of view will appear from another angle to be the outworking of a plan in which God is in full control.

Jacob failed to do two things: he failed to take into account the possibility that he had made a miscalculation. Unbelief assumes a certainty of its own. Jacob was res-olute in his despair. He "refused to be comforted" (Gen. 37:35). No amount of "what if" caveats could shake him. Gloom took on a life of its own and spiraled into the blackness of the land of despair.

More importantly, he also failed to reckon into his equation the invisible hand of God. And that is always a fatal mistake. God's ways are mysterious: they are often hidden to our sensory world of perception. To cite the remaining stanzas of William Cowper's hymn "God Moves in a Mysterious Way":

> Deep in unfathomable mines
> Of never-failing skill
> He treasures up his bright designs
> And works his sovereign will.
>
> Blind unbelief is sure to err
> And scan his work in vain;
> God is his own interpreter,
> And he will make it plain.

God was *for* Jacob in the same sense that the psalmist can say, "God is *for* me" (Ps. 56:9). Paul seems to be borrowing the phrase in the grand expanse of Romans, culminating in the cry—*Deus pro nobis*, "God is *for* us" (Rom. 8:31). God had a plan for Jacob and his family revealed by way of covenant with Jacob's father and grandfather. The purpose of God to save his people for eternity was bound up with the survival of Joseph and Simeon! There was no way for God to abandon his promise. The "facts" staring Jacob in the face *had to be interpreted in another way*. God was in the details—the details that Jacob could not see.

What this says to us is that no matter how dark things may appear to be, we must reckon with the invisible hand of God that works all things—yes, "all things" for our good (Rom 8:28). As God's children, we may not always appreciate *what* it is that God may be doing in our lives; but we are to trust that in every aspect of it God is fulfilling the best of plans that ultimately will be for our good. The alternative is too terrible to contemplate: things may contrive to negate the hand of God and ensure our doom. No! That can never be!

At the heart of this view of providence, then, is the need to place our trust entirely into his government and care. We need to learn to say, along with the hymn writer Samuel Rodigast, "Whate'er My God Ordains Is Right," originally penned in the seventeenth century:

> Whate'er my God ordains is right:
> His holy will abideth;
> I will be still whate'er he doth;
> And follow where he guideth;
> He is my God; though dark my road,
> He holds me that I shall not fall:
> Wherefore to him I leave it all.
>
> Whate'er my God ordains is right:
> He is my Friend and Father;
> He suffers naught to do me harm,
> Though many storms may gather,
> Now I may know both joy and woe,
> Some day I shall see clearly
> That he hath loved me dearly.
> Whate'er my God ordains is right:
> Though now this cup, in drinking,
> May bitter seem to my faint heart,
> I take it, all unshrinking.
> My God is true; each morn anew

Sweet comfort yet shall fill my heart,
And pain and sorrow shall depart.[27]

REDEMPTIVE PROVIDENCE

There is one final consideration of providence that should occupy us: the One who governs and ensures the good outcome is our Redeemer. The Mediator has achieved redemption for us. He has been glorified because he has finished the work that he was given to do (John 17:4-5). He has been exalted because he has been obedient unto death (Phil. 2:8-9). And he exercises his rule *in the interests of his people*; he is "head over all things to the church" (Eph. 1:22). All authority is given to him (Matt. 28:18). Whatever the current lethargy of the contemporary church, it is a situation that is entirely known to our Savior, and his determination is undiminished to "present the church to himself in splendor, without spot or wrinkle or any such thing, that she might be holy and without blemish" (Eph. 5:27). His kingdom is coming and *will come!* God will ensure the fulfillment of his designs *for the sake of his Son.* He has asked for the nations as his heritage and they will be given to him (Ps. 2:8). Out of the anguish of his soul, he will be satisfied (Isa. 53:11).

No matter what circumstance we may find ourselves in, we may always be assured that it is covered by the efficacy of the atoning blood of Jesus Christ. The cross dispels any doubt as to the outcome, for there—in the darkest point of human history—sin and evil were conquered and Satan vanquished. In the strictest sense, everything is converging so as to bring glory to the triune God. Nothing, absolutely nothing is adrift of the purposes of God to accomplish his ultimate design for the cosmos. In the famous words of Abraham Kuyper given at the inaugural address at the opening of the Free University, Amsterdam: "There is not a square inch in the whole domain of human existence over which Christ, who is sovereign over *all*, does not cry, 'Mine!' "[28]

NOTES

1 Augustine, "Enchiridion" Chap. 96, in *Nicene and Post-Nicene Fathers* (First Series), vol. 3, *St. Augustin: On the Holy Trinity. Doctrinal Treatises, Moral Treatises*, ed. Philip Schaff (Peabody, MA: Hendrickson, 2004), 267.

2 For example, God does not speak to us as he did to Abraham or Moses. And the fact that miracles are not evenly distributed in the history of redemption, confined as they seem to be to periods of massive divine revelation in the lifetime of the patriarchs, the prophets Elijah and Elisha, and the dawning of the new covenant era, should lead us to be cautious (at the very least) of suggesting similar phenomena in our time.

3 We may defy God and reject his plan, but this, too, is part of his plan. One part of his plan is the judgment of sin. Those who reject this part of God's plan for salvation through Jesus Christ fulfill another—they choose a dark eternity and God respects that choice. This also is part of the plan.

4 These lines are taken from the hymn, "God Moves in a Mysterious Way," originally given the title, "Light Shining out of Darkness" in William Cowper (1731-1800) and John Newton (1725-1807), *Olney Hymns*, Book 3, Hymn 15.

5 John Flavel, "Navigation Spiritualized: Or, A New Compass for Seamen," *Works* (1820; Edinburgh: The Banner of Truth Trust, 1968), 4:284.

6 The Westminster Confession of Faith (1646), 5.1.

7 *Hamlet*, act 5, scene 2, line 10.

8 Harold S. Kushner, *When Bad Things Happen to Good People* (New York: Avon Books, 1983), 43.

9 Gregory Boyd, *God at War: The Bible and Spiritual Conflict* (Downers Grove, IL.: InterVarsity Press, 1997), 20. Boyd has also written elsewhere: "God simply can't override free wills whenever they might conflict with his will. Because God decided to create this kind of world, he can't ensure that his will is carried out in every situation. He must tolerate and wisely work around the irrevocable freedom of human and spirit agents." Gregory A. Boyd, *Is God to Blame?* (Downers Grove, IL: InterVarsity Press, 2003), 125.

10. Jonathan Edwards, *The Freedom of the Will*, 2.12 (1845; Morgan, PA: Soli Deo Gloria, 1996), 134.

11 John Calvin, *Institutes of the Christian Religion*, ed. John T. McNeill, trans. Ford Lewis Battles (Philadelphia: Westminster Press, 1960), 1:201.

12 William Hasker, *God, Time, and Knowledge* (Ithaca, NY: Cornell University Press, 1989), 57-58.

13 Middle knowledge has been the subject of intense discussion and analysis by the Christian philosopher Alvin Plantinga in *The Nature of Necessity* (Oxford: Clarendon Press, 1974).

14 William Lane Craig, *The Only Wise God* (Grand Rapids: Baker, 1987), 135.

15 For an analysis of this problem, see Paul Helm, *The Providence of God* (Leicester: Inter-Varsity Press, 1993), 55-61. Molinism does not, of course, "solve" the problem of human freedom entirely, since we are still left wondering why

this set of human choices was "chosen" rather than any other set.

16 William Hasker, *God, Time, and Knowledge*, 187. Cited by James S. Spiegel, *The Benefits of Providence: A New Look at Divine Sovereignty* (Wheaton, IL: Crossway, 2005), 41.

17 Boyd, *God at War*, 20.

18 Boyd, *Is God to Blame?* 91.

19 As Hasker puts it, "predictions based on foresight drawn from existing trends and tendencies." *God, Time, and Knowledge*, 194.

20 The reference to the doctrine of penal substitution as "a form of cosmic child-abuse" made in *The Lost Message of Jesus* by Steve Chalke and Alan Mann has, understandably, provoked a flurry of responses. For the original comment, see Steve Chalke and Alan Mann, *The Lost Message of Jesus* (Grand Rapids: Zondervan, 2003), 182. For a response, see Steve Jeffrey, Mike Ovey, and Andrew Sach, *Pierced for Our Transgressions* (Nottingham: Inter-Varsity Press, 2007).

21 The understanding of "all sinned" in verse 12 must be understood as one of solidarity with Adam rather than personal, voluntary sin on our part. For an analysis of Romans 5:12-21, see John Murray, *The Imputation of Adam's Sin* (Philadelphia: Presbyterian & Reformed, 1959).

22 Augustine, *Enchiridion*, XI.

23 C. H. Spurgeon, *Morning and Evening*, reading for the morning of August 5.

24 Jerry Bridges, *Is God Really in Control? Trusting God in a World of Hurt* (Colorado Springs, CO: NavPress, 2006), 69-70.

25 C. S. Lewis, *Miracles* (1947; New York: Touchstone, 1996), 232.

26 *Inferno*, 3.7.

27 The hymn was translated by Catherine Winkworth in the nineteenth century.

28 The address was given on October 20, 1880. For the whole address, see "Sphere Sovereignty," in *Abraham Kuyper: A Centennial Reader*, ed. James D. Bratt (Grand Rapids: Eerdmans, 1998), 463-90. The quotation itself comes near the end of the address; see page 488.